Wherefore Art Thou?
A Kid's Guide To Verona, Italy

Photography By John D. Weigand
Poetry By Penelope Dyan

Bellissima Publishing, LLC
Jamul, California
www.bellissimapublishing.com

copyright © 2010 by Penny D. Weigand

All rights reserved. No part of this book may be
reproduced or transmitted in any form or by any means,
electronic or mechanical, including photocopying,
recording, or by any other means, or by any information or
storage retrieval system, without permission from the publisher.

ISBN 978-1-935630-32-6

First Edition

Wherefore Art Thou?
Bellissima Publishing, LLC

Introduction

The tragic play, Romeo and Juliet, was written early in the career of William Shakespeare. It is the tale of two young star-crossed lovers whose deaths finally unite their feuding families. It was one of Shakespeare's most popular plays.

The story takes place in Verona where you can go and see for yourself where Juliet and her family lived, and just a short walk away from Juliet's house is the house where Romeo lived with his family. The people of Verona will tell you they aren't sure if the story of Romeo and Juliet is true, but they are quite sure the families existed; and that there was indeed a feud between them. It is sad to think the two young lovers had to die to bring the families together and to stop the feud, but it is a tale that has withstood time; and there is definitely a lesson to be learned in it. Shakespeare's Romeo and Juliet plot is actually based on an Italian tale, translated into verse, "The Tragical History of Romeus and Juliet" by Arthur Brooke, written in 1562, and retold in prose in William Painter's "Palace of Pleasure" in 1582.

Since this is a tale of antiquity, there is a likelihood there is an element of truth in it. This is why John D. Weigand and Penelope Dyan traveled all the way to Verona. . . to decide for themselves if the tale was true. What did they decide? They decided to let you decide. So walk through the beautiful streets of Verona, Italy with them and see what you think. One thing is certain, the lesson in the tale is timeless. Use this book to introduce your child to both Verona and Shakespeare and feel confident in its purpose, as Dyan is a former K-12, teacher, an attorney and an award winning author who really understands kids!

Wherefore Art Thou?
A Kid's Guide To Verona, Italy

Photography By John D. Weigand
Poetry By Penelope Dyan

*It was William Shakespeare, or so it is said,
who retold an old tale out of his head.
No one knows if the story is true,
so we shall leave the determination of that all up to you.*

It was in Verona, such a beautiful place,
where lived young Juliet, so fair of face.
You can see her in her garden at wait.
Will her Romeo appear at yonder gate?

And here on the streets of Verona, pray tell,
lovers walk past the house wherein Romeo dwelled.
Romeo and Juliet tried as they might,
to escape to togetherness through dark of night.
Secretly married, and yet still apart,
Romeo and Juliet were together, one heart.

And as Juliet stood on the balcony above,
Romeo called up to his one true love.
For Romeo, Juliet was the sun and the moon,
and he prayed with his heart they would together be soon.

"Romeo, Romeo, wherefore art thou Romeo?"
Juliet cried out from above. . .

As she looked down from that balcony to see her true love.

Inside fair Juliet's house all were asleep.

The beauty of their love was a secret they'd keep.

Not even the remnants of the home's hearth's fire could ever compare to their love's true desire.

And in the house you can still see Juliet's bed,
where once she lay her lovely head.

You leave Juliet's house and you wonder why,
these lovers so tragically had to die?
It was all because of a family feud,
Although it seems senseless, you leave, hope renewed.
Perhaps Shakespeare's story was truly pretend,
but the message of this story will never end.
And as you gaze in silence off afar,
you wonder where Romeo and Juliet are.

And if they see, after all,
the lovers' messages upon the wall.
Written on the walls and everywhere for you to see
just how important and serious true love can be...
And how extremely dangerous can be hate,
if it gets beyond your garden's gate.

As you walk the streets where Juliet once walked,
you can stop and hear the people talk.
It is of William Shakespeare's tale they have heard.
Some even know it word for word.

And as you pause and look around,
at all the beauty that does abound.
You will wonder if the tale is true.
You will wonder if this could happen to you.
Then your mother will say, "It is not right,
for anyone to feud or fight."
You will smile because your mother is kind,
and also because she can read your mind.

As you approach Romeo's front door,
You'll remember dear Romeo lives there there no more.
And now you know. . . oh so well. . .
about the story of Verona that Shakespeare did tell.
And you have seen the very place,
where Romeo and Juliet once stood face to face.
You'll wonder as you stand there at Juliet's gate,
why they had to meet their destiny's tragic fate.
Love does not always conquer all.
Sometimes love and innocence has to fall.
But it doesn't have to be this way
if we live in harmony day after day.
If we live lives of goodness one day at a time,
Or lives will most surely be sublime!